Just You and I

Devotions from the Heart

Novia Reid

Note to readers: The author is not engaged in rendering professional advice of any kind in this book. This book is not intended to be and is not a substitute for professional help.

Gratitude

Thank you, God, for whispering your purpose to me and entrusting me to pour into your daughters. To my parents, sisters, mentors, and friends who encouraged, empowered, and supported me— thank you so much. Warmest thanks to Levan Warner and Iris Errar for their time, effort, and invaluable insights toward this book. And, to every woman who reads this devotional, I dedicate it to you.

Preface

One day, while reading a devotional, God whispered to me, "that will be you one day." I laughed in my spirit, but later I embraced what I heard and embarked on a journey to write a devotional that would enrich, uplift, and strengthen women as the one I'd read had done for me. Thus, Just You and I Devotions from the Heart was written. My prayer is that this devotional will bless and change your life.

Divinely Designed

I will praise You, for I am fearfully and wonderfully made; marvelous are Your works, and that my soul knows very well.

Psalm 139:14

Sometimes it is hard to envision about ourselves what Christ sees, but if we did, we would stand amazed! While we might look at ourselves and see someone unworthy, unloved, and unblessed, Christ views us in a different light. In His eyes, we are priceless jewels, loved unreservedly, and highly favored.

In His eyes, you are extraordinary! There is absolutely nothing in the world He would trade you for. He made you and is proud to declare you as His daughter. He feels no embarrassment or guilt in claiming you. Your existence brings joy to His heart.

You were thought of with precision and exuberance. You are *divinely designed* by God—abundant time was taken to create you! The beauty of your smile is flawless, and you have the heart of an innocent child. The ability to nurture and persuade are gifts you possess. A deep resilience is within you that allows you to rise above challenges and display gentleness and meekness with coveted grace.

An unbelievable power lies within you. Do you know the power that is in your words, your smile, your heart, your mind, and your character? Recognize within yourself whom God designed—a woman who is divinely designed. Give God praise for being a woman. Give Him praise for you!

~

Remember, you are divinely designed.

Using each letter of your first name, write something good about yourself.

Creative Writing

~ Just You and I ~

There Are Blessings in Forgiveness

"For if you forgive men their trespasses, your heavenly Father will also forgive you."

Matthew 6:14

Writer, producer, and actor, Tyler Perry, has become a household name. He has produced movies, plays, and sitcoms with powerful themes that have captured people's hearts globally. One of his moving films portrays the importance of forgiving others, thus allowing God to forgive and restore us.

Diary of a Mad Black Woman revealed the journey of a woman who was abused, degraded, and dishonored during her marriage. She tried her best to be a good wife, but her husband did all he could to destroy her spirit. After many years of marriage, her husband left her for another woman. Her heart was broken and infused with anger.

After enduring emotional turmoil, with encouragement from her mother, she allowed God to teach, mold, and heal her. Eventually, she made a difficult but worthy decision. She forgave her husband.

Forgiveness is not agreeing with what has happened to you, trusting the person who hurt you again, or restoring the friendship or relationship you once had. Forgiveness is accepting what occurred while acknowledging that what occurred doesn't define you. Forgiveness is releasing yourself from any negative emotion attached to your experience, which means letting go of the guilt, regret, and shame and embracing what and who remains following the lessons you have learned.

Jesus says to forgive, that you may receive forgiveness (Mark 11:26). Forgiving those who have wronged, hurt, or abandoned us is not an easily traveled road. Conquering pain and hurt is difficult. It requires time and the ability to allow God to help us. Sometimes our ability to forgive is tested, but in the end, forgiveness benefits us.

Forgiveness brings joy, relief, and inner peace. Power comes back to us when we forgive. What happened to us no longer consumes our minds, hearts, and souls. We move forward. If ever uncertainty arises about the reasons to forgive, remind yourself—there are blessings in forgiveness—*for you.*

Remember, there are blessings in forgiveness.

Is there someone you need to forgive? Ask God to help you.

Creative Writing

~ Just You and I ~

It's Just You and I

"God is Spirit, and those who worship Him must worship in spirit and truth."

John 4:24

The book of John says *worship must be done in spirit and truth.* What is God saying to us? Our thoughts, the focus of our hearts, and desires, reflect worship.

When you are in the realm of worship, no music is needed. It is pure intimacy between you and God. He holds you, comforts you, and speaks to you in ways He knows you will understand. When you are in worship with God, you are naked before Him in truth. You don't hide. There is total transparency. All your imperfections are present yet *accepted.*

God shares with you. You share with Him. Nothing can come between your intimate moments with Him. Can you be counted as a true worshipper of God? Wonderful for you and me, God has made it clear what He desires from us. You can worship Him and with Him each day. He loves your worship, and there is no limit to the fulfilment you can experience.

Your worship is understood and desired by God. It is vital to your relationship with Him. Therefore, worship Him *in spirit and truth*!

Remember the last time you had worship with the Lord.

Spend daily moments with God in worship.

Creative Writing

~ Just You and I ~

Kind Strangers

"Let your light so shine before men, that they may see your good works and glorify your Father in heaven."

Matthew 5:16

At age two, I was the recipient of a precious gift given by the kindest strangers—I was offered a second chance at life. You see, I was not expected to live beyond my teenage years, but God intervened on my behalf. At six weeks old, I was diagnosed with a heart murmur that my doctor thought I would outgrow.

I did not outgrow it. For almost two years, the severity of my condition was unnoticed until I began to tire easily, become short of breath and my skin would become blue. A visit to a specialist confirmed I had tetralogy of Fallot—a condition that could only be fixed with open heart surgery. At that time, no doctor in Jamaica performed that type of operation. Without it, the doctor informed my parents, I only had a few weeks to live.

My parents had no idea what to do. They didn't have enough money or assets, but God sent help through a kind doctor. She, my eldest sister, and others advocated for me and worked tirelessly to help. Their hard work paid off as Yale New Haven Hospital in Connecticut agreed to perform my surgery, while Variety Clubs International offered to cover the surgery expenses and Air Jamaica graciously stepped in and paid the airfare for my mother and me. It would be our first trip to the United States.

The surgeon and his wonderful team performed a six-hour operation to repair my heart. The hospital only charged $3,500. Nearly $18,000 worth of services was donated by these kind strangers to save my life. That amount may seem inexpensive now, but it was not in those days. I stand in awe at the limitless blessings in my story. God used these strangers in an incredible way. He used them to help save my life.

We have the choice to be kind to everyone—even strangers. Be kind and tenderhearted to one another, for the kind deed of a stranger can change someone's life.

I credit the details of this story to my parents, Norma and Lindsay Reid, and staff reporter Joan Barbuto.

Remember, you can make a difference in a stranger's life.

Pray for a stranger today.

Creative Writing

~ Just You and I ~

Jesus Is Everything You Need

"I am the Alpha and the Omega, the Beginning and the End, the First and the Last."

Revelation 22:13

Jesus,

A widow finds comfort in Your words and in Your arms.
A saddened heart is cheered by You.
With one touch from You, pieces of a broken heart are mended.
The power of Your healing is indescribable.
Your sweet voice restores hope in the heart of a motherless child.
The whisper of Your voice soothes a grieving mother's heart.
The peace You give surpasses all understanding.
Your words are food to the hungry soul.
On one's darkest days, You are a ray of sunshine.
A hopeless person has hope of a purposeful life because of You.
You minister to the lost, the wealthy, and the poor.
The forgotten of the world are remembered by You.
The love You express is for all.
A life spent in sin—You can restore.
A perfect lover You are.

Jesus, You are the Alpha and the Omega, the Beginning, and the End, the First and the Last!
There is no one like You.

Remember: Jesus is everything you need.

Sing a song of praise to Jesus for who He is.

Creative Writing

This Is Your Season

To everything there is a season, a time for every purpose under heaven.

Ecclesiastes 3:1

It's a new season, filled with many possibilities.
Fulfill your dreams.
Be inspired!

Give thanks and praise to God in this season, despite your circumstances.
Let praise be your custom.
Share your praise.
Be content in all things.
Hope in God.

Celebrate the woman you are now and destined to be.
Love yourself—past, mistakes, flaws, character, beauty, and all.
Embrace your body.
Embrace your scars.

It is a brand-new season!

This is your season to exercise faith like you never have before.

This is another season to live, love, and laugh!

Remember to make the most of every season.

Write down one goal you would like to accomplish in this season.

Creative Writing

~ Just You and I ~

At His Appointed Time

Rest in the Lord, and wait patiently for Him.

Psalm 37:7a

The story of Lazarus draws our attention to the frustration, hurt, confusion, and disappointment that we feel when Jesus does not show up when we believe that we need Him most. If we are honest, sometimes we are angry, enraged even, and we throw a tantrum because, in our eyes, Jesus failed. Often, He seemingly intervenes at a time that we believe is too late.

We struggle to understand why Jesus does not act when we desire Him to, and we are left to grapple with a truth in Scripture that says God's ways are not our ways. Again, if we are being honest, that verse, even if we usually believe it, sometimes does little to soothe us in our distress. Yet, this truth can ease our distress and bring us comfort and hope when we embrace its meaning.

Jesus waited four days to raise Lazarus from the dead, and this fact reveals another truth that we may know but struggle to accept— Jesus has an appointed time for a good reason. *We never wait in vain.* Lazarus had been in a tomb for four days, and his body had decomposed. His organs, muscles, and joints were no longer functioning. Only a miracle would raise him from the dead, and people witnessed what they needed to see. That was Jesus' purpose—

He wanted people to believe, to trust Him. He desired to encourage them, restore their hope, draw them closer to Him, and save them through faith.

Here is another truth: God's divinity and perfect purpose will always outweigh our desire for instant relief and pleasure. While we seek immediate alleviation of our suffering, God's ways reflect a deeper intention. His focus lies with refining our character, bringing our destinies to life, and saving us and others.

His appointed time serves you and me, even when it doesn't feel or seem like it. So, when it doesn't feel or seem like it, God understands, and He is patient. God knows you won't understand it all at the moment. However, I do pray that you allow the dust to clear and the anger, disappointment, and frustration to heal, and you witness the love of God during what in your eyes seems like a delay.

Remember, at God's appointed time, all things will come together for your good.

Pray for patience.

Creative Writing

Welcome Home

"And when he comes home, he calls together his friends and neighbors, saying to them, 'Rejoice with me, for I have found my sheep which was lost!'"

Luke 15:6

Mothers have felt the heartbreak and disappointment from their child choosing to leave or run away from home. The heart of these mothers beat fast and worry about their child occupies their minds. They worry if their child is clothed, fed, and safe. It's hard for them to rest.

At times, these mothers' dreams come true, and their child returns home. What a hard decision that must be for them amidst the likely feelings of guilt, shame, regret, and fear. Yet despite their emotions, the brave decision to go home is made.

God experiences a deeper pain when you, His daughter, wander away for Him. He is concerned about you, whether you are clothed, fed, safe, and in alignment with His will. God still watches over you because your decisions do not influence His character or love for you. But would He prefer you to be home, in alignment with His will and fellowship with Him? Absolutely.

God is patient so He will wait for you, but He won't leave you alone. The uneasiness you feel, the severance of relationships, the heartbreak—sometimes what happens to you is God trying to get your attention because He wants you home. There is no place like home, and you belong in the safety of God. You belong in alignment with His will, and you are meant to live a holy, abundant, joyful, and purposed life.

If you are out of alignment with God's will for your life, please, go home. If you are living an unholy life, please, go home. If you are lost, please, go home. Going home means surrendering your life and your will to God. There is no better place to be than in the will and presence of God.

Resist the enemy's lie that you are too far gone to save. Resist his lie that you are too deep in your addiction or sin for God to reach down and pull you out. Resist his lie that God no longer loves you or wants you because of your mistakes. Resist his lies and bravely go home. God is waiting for you, and when you go home, God's response will be, daughter *welcome home.*

Remember, God will always welcome you home.

Return to God if you need to.

Creative Writing

~ Just You and I ~

You Are Someone's Encouragement

Be kindly affectionate to one another with brotherly love, in honor giving preference to one another.

Romans 12:10

We all need support and encouragement in different aspects of our lives. No one person is an island. Sometimes, we need a shoulder to cry on, advice, or financial help.

Here is a story from my dear friend, Yanique Deane, that I hope encourages you:

"I'd like to take you back to a day in college. One morning I woke up, ready to start my day, and I realized that there was no food in my refrigerator. I checked my bank account and had only one dollar. I said, "God, I have no food to eat, but I am going to praise you anyhow." I went about my day and visited my advisor, whom I was very close with at the time. She was on her way out the door when I arrived and she asked me to accompany her to Target. I went along with her, and she advised me that she was making a gift basket consisting of food for an employee. I helped her choose what to place in the basket. When we arrived back on campus, she dropped me off at my dorm and asked me to meet her at the office later that day. And so, I did. At this point, I was very hungry; however, she was not aware of this. I went to her office later that day,

where she presented me with the gift basket that I had helped her create. I cried, and I looked up to the sky and thanked God. I had enough food to last me a month. She did not know it, but she had encouraged me. Her act brought tears to my eyes and happiness in my heart."

You are someone else's encouragement. Never think what you do or say does not matter. You matter, and what you bring to this world matters. The encouragement that someone is looking for rests within you. So, do what you do best and be someone's encouragement.

Special thanks to Yanique for sharing her story.

Remember, an encouraging word, smile, or deed can brighten someone's life.

Encourage someone today.

Creative Writing

Consistency Has Power

"For I am the Lord, I do not change."

Malachi 3:6a

When I think of the verse in Malachi chapter three, the word consistent comes to mind. God has many attributes, but one of His most beloved characteristics is His consistency. In a world where our hearts, desires, friendships, and relationships change, sometimes swiftly, it is comforting to know that the One who has the authority and justification to be inconsistent chooses to be consistent.

God's consistency is a choice. That fact alone speaks to His love for us. When we choose sin over holiness, break our vows to God and others, or stray from His will, God's character does not waver. Your sins, even those you believe are unforgivable are forgiven. That's consistency.

Like God, we can be consistent. Despite our shortcomings, mistakes, and sins, we can make a conscious decision to be consistent in our devotion to God. We can commit to walking in holiness. We can choose to love our enemies.

Being consistent does not mean we ignore our bodies when it tells us to rest or push past our pain instead of seeking to heal it. Being consistent is always taking care of ourselves and being our best selves, whatever our best is, and understanding that our "best" looks differently when we're healthy than it does when we are ill. We can be consistent by choosing to keep showing up for our dreams when progress is slow and when God says "wait" to our prayers. We can choose consistency by being patient with our children and ourselves when tempted to be intolerant.

Consistency is for us. Our consistency fortifies our character, honors God, and is a key to success and inner peace. Consistency builds maturity and resilience. Consistency is a choice, and while it is not always an easy one, through the Holy Spirit, we can be consistent.

Remember: God does not change.

Reflect on areas of your life in which you can become more consistent.

Creative Writing

A Touch of Faith

So Jesus said to them, "Because of your unbelief; for assuredly, I say to you, if you have faith as a mustard seed, you will say to this mountain, 'Move from here to there,' and it will move; and nothing will be impossible for you."

Matthew 17:20

Jesus says faith as a mustard seed is all you need, and nothing will be impossible for you. The size of a mustard seed is that of a dot (·) from a pencil point. Jesus could have asked for faith the size of a mountain or as steadfast as Abraham's. Instead, He says to us that if we have just a little faith, our mountains can move.

No earthly physician had been able to heal or cure a woman who bled for twelve years. When she heard of Jesus, she believed He could heal her. Within her heart she said, "If only I may touch His clothes, I shall be made well" (Mark 5:28). Read Jesus' response to the woman's touch. Jesus didn't say that His touch healed her. Jesus said, "Daughter, thy faith hath made thee whole" (Mark 5:34). Her faith healed her.

This woman shows us two important keys of faith: alignment and readiness. Her words matched her actions. She believed in her heart Jesus could heal her with one touch and she affirmed that belief by pushing through the crowd to touch Him. Your words and actions must be in alignment. The other key of her faith was readiness. When Jesus passed by, she was in position to be healed. Be in position for Jesus to answer your prayer.

Now, in a moment of transparency, you could probably attest that even with genuine, mustard seed faith, there has been a time or two when what you prayed for did not happen. In situations like these, your faith is still necessary. However, your faith is now needed in God's providence and love for you, believing that both are present when He says no or wait. Though you may not always love God's answers when you have exercised true faith, be pleased that you kept the faith.

R*emember, your mustard seed faith can move mountains.*

A*sk God to remove anything that is hindering your faith.*

Creative Writing

Everything Matters to Jesus

"But the very hairs of your head are all numbered."
Matthew 10:30

May this poem affirm how concerned Jesus is about every area of your life.

When the bus or taxi leaves you and you tried your hardest to be on time, I am sorry.
When your friend has hurt you with words, I hurt too.
When you are nervous at your job interview, I am your peace.
When you are exhausted but must work, I am your strength.
When you feel your mistakes are too grave to be forgiven, remember the cross.

If your husband has left you, I will stay by your side.
If you are nervous to sing for fear of being out of tune, know your voice is beautiful to Me.
If you are laid off, I will supply your needs.
If you are timid to express your feelings, I will give you the confidence to speak.
If the keys to your vehicle are lost, I will guide you to them.
If you are torn between silk or suede, I will help you decide. In either, you look stunning!

In times you want to read My word but aren't certain where to start, I will guide you.
In moments you want to shed a tear, I am near, so weep freely.
In moments you feel insecure, find affirmation in My word.
In times you wonder where I am, I am always near. I will never leave you nor forsake you.
In situations when you feel like giving up, hold on—I will come through.

Remember, Jesus is concerned about everything that has to do with you.
Entrust every part of your life to Jesus.

Creative Writing

~ Just You and I ~

The God Who Heals

Then your light shall break forth like the morning, your healing shall spring forth speedily, and your righteousness shall go before you.

Isaiah 58:8a

There will never be enough room in one book to write the stories of women who have been hurt and need healing. We all have been hurt. There are times we try to escape our hurt by traveling to new places, burying ourselves into our work or church role, or entertaining casual relationships. We may not realize that running, instead of confronting our pain, creates a heart that is harder to heal.

We cannot escape our hurt, no matter how or what we try. Our best remedy for a hurt and broken heart is to heal it. There are times when God heals us by Himself and depression ends, the stark pain of divorce is erased, and we forgive ourselves for our mistakes. Your heart, mind, and soul are transformed, and you are empowered to live a holy, prosperous, purposed life. Malachi (4:2a) declares, "But to you who fear My name, the Son of Righteousness shall arise with healing in His wings!"

Rest assured, despite the hurt that you have endured, God can heal you. There is no trauma, sin, or illness that He cannot heal by Himself. Yet there are times God desires to use someone to help you heal. His reasons are unique to every woman. What is most important is not how the healing occurs, but that you remain open to healing.

God never intended pain to be your final fate. Your hurt was not meant to last forever. God wants you to heal and wants to see you healed. Your affliction, which is but for a moment, is working for you a far more exceeding and eternal weight of glory (2 Corinthians 4:17)! Your healing is available. Be willing to pursue it and experience every good thing that comes from a woman that is truly healed.

Remember, you can heal.

Ask God to show you your path to healing.

Creative Writing

The Sword of the Spirit

Your word is a lamp to my feet and a light to my path.
Psalm 119:105

As a youth who studied books of the Bible for competitions, I grew accustomed to reading about the diverse genealogies, tribes, and customs throughout the Old Testament. Then and later in my young adult life, some verses and chapters were uninteresting, thus causing drowsiness and leading me to close the Bible sooner than I likely should have. However, as I matured in my knowledge of God and the relevance of His word, I realized that even the most seemingly mundane or unimportant verse has a purpose that should be regarded, and not discarded as irrelevant.

You see, I have come to know that God is intentional. Nothing He says or does is by chance. No. Everything has a purpose which leads me to believe that every word in the Bible was willfully included and serves a purpose for us. Our duty is to be willing to seek God's intention for us and our lives from His word. Our priority is not completing a yearly Bible plan so we can check it off our lists or reading an entire chapter to satisfy our commitment to study the word of God every day. Rather, our focus should be a genuine interest to understand God's purpose and message for us, whether in one verse, a passage, or chapter.

Transformation happens, not when reading the Bible is viewed as a religious obligation, but when we seek God's wisdom with a sincere and purposed heart. There have been moments when *one* verse was God's direct message to me, whether a message of hope, encouragement, insight about His character or providence or direction for my life. One verse! And there have been moments when a verse challenged me to correct an attitude or behavior, step out of my comfort zone, and minister in a way I never anticipated. There have been times when a few verses served as the cornerstone for a sermon. This is the power of God's word.

The direction, hope, wisdom, and help that you seek is embedded in God's holy word. Everything you need to travel this road called life is in it. In Ephesians, Paul describes the Bible as part of the armor of God that we need to fight spiritual warfare. Everything you want to know about the powerful, merciful, and loving God, the good and kind Savior, everything about redemption is in the Bible. I encourage you to carve out time to read God's word, to become intimate with God's thoughts of you, purpose for you, love toward you, and direction for your everyday life. Read it and you will grasp why it transforms lives the way it does.

Remember: the Bible is a lamp to your feet and a light to your path.

Commit to read the Bible daily (a verse, passage, or chapter).

Creative Writing

The Intentional Encounter

"For thus says the Lord God: Indeed I Myself will search for My sheep and seek them out."

Ezekiel 34: 13

Jesus wanted and intended to meet the Samaritan woman at the well. While other Jews chose an alternate and longer route solely to avoid the Samaritans, Jesus took the direct route to meet and connect with her. Their encounter was intentional.

Jesus sought and found her when He knew she would be alone. At noon, the heat was unbearable, however, many people would likely not see her then. Thus, she would not be subject to condemnation, chastisement, or gossip about being married five times and involved with a man who was not her husband. Sometimes, we reduce intentional divine encounters to simple coincidences because we do not realize or perhaps believe that God is purposeful in seeking us out.

Open your eyes to see how Jesus is seeking you and what He is drawing your attention to. The Samaritan's woman willingness to engage in a seemingly ordinary, mundane conversation led to her awareness that she was speaking to the Messiah. Jesus revealed Himself to her, and that encounter changed her life. Their meeting was intentional, and Jesus' intentionality extends to you. He is intentional about knowing you intimately, meeting you in your suffering, healing you from sin, and giving you eternal life. Open your eyes and heart to see his willfulness toward you, which stems solely from unconditional love.

You are not an inconvenience to God. He made you with intention, and you remain on this earth for a specific purpose. Therefore, understand that God's actions in your life are purposeful and meaningful. He will seek you out, wherever you are, in whatever condition you are in.

Remember, Jesus is intentional about you.

Be intentional in seeking Jesus.

Creative Writing

~ Just You and I ~

Let Praise Be Your Custom

From the rising of the sun to its going down the
Lord's name is to be praised.

Psalm 113:3

Jesus dying on calvary is reason enough for us to praise God for the rest of our lives. Yet the reality of our lives sometimes stifles our praise and produces fear, worry, and anxiety, which I understand. But, amidst my darkest and most challenging experiences, I have realized that praise is a remedy. Praise heals. Praise feels good to the soul. Praise unlocks God's favor, and praise renews our strength in God. So, my encouragement to you is to let praise be your custom.

The boat called life will rock. Praise God anyhow.
Friends will walk away. Praise God anyhow.
When your loved one dies, praise God's name.
Hurt will come. Praise God anyhow.
Lonely nights may come. Praise God anyhow.
People may take advantage of you. Praise God still.
When your faith becomes weary, praise God anyhow.
If your relationships are struggling, still praise God.

When God gives you instructions that you don't understand,
praise Him anyhow.
If you have an illness, praise God.
If you lose your home, praise God.
When the devil tries to steal your joy, give God all the praise.
When you are tempted to lose your praise, praise God anyhow!

Remember, let praise be your custom.

Listen to the song "I Never Lost My Praise" by Tramaine Hawkins.

Creative Writing

~ Just You and I ~

Give Your Best, Always

Therefore, whether you eat or drink, or whatever you do, do all to the glory of God.

1 Corinthians 10:31

From washing the dishes to chaperoning a field trip to delivering a keynote at Harvard University, every task is worthy. And I believe in giving our best to every task we are given and pursue. Giving our best is being fully present, engaged, attentive to what we are doing, and completing our tasks with a positive attitude, passion, and effort.

Some tasks may be mundane, and we may dread them. But dreading them creates misery and affects our result. God calls us to do everything with all our hearts and minds. As every detail of our lives matters to Him, every task we do should matter to us and be revered. Give your best, always.

However, understand this, your best will not always look the same. Your best may look different if you are sick or mentally drained. Sometimes, giving your best to your assignment means reprioritizing, saying no to something else, or letting go of some obligations. Sometimes, giving your best means pausing to do some deep breathing.

Sometimes, that means checking in with yourself and asking, "girl, how are you?" Sometimes, that means turning off your cellphone for twenty minutes and resting. Sometimes, that means a weekend getaway with your friends. In other times, it means sneaking away to your special prayer place to connect with God, even if it's just to say, I need You.

Giving your best is not about perfection or making yourself available for everyone and saying yes to every request. It's giving your best effort, whatever that is, always. In everything you do, God wants you to be purposeful. He does not want you to burn out. That is not His desire or will for you, but He wants you to do everything at your best.

Remember to give your best, always.

Consider an action that you may need to take so you can give your best to God.

Creative Writing

~ Just You and I ~

God's Grace Is Enough

And He said to me, "My grace is sufficient for you, for My strength is made perfect in weakness."

2 Corinthians 12:9a

Women are battling to let go of the sins and mistakes of their past. Some women may have heard, and some may believe that they do not deserve forgiveness and will never be whole. Reminiscing about their mistakes and sins keeps them from moving forward.

Here are two salient truths: you can move forward, and God wants you to move forward. We all have a history, and, in that history, we have fallen short many times of doing what is righteous. We have said and done some things that we are not proud of. We have sometimes fallen below the standards we have set for ourselves. We have sometimes let God down.

Still, God says this to you, His daughter, "my grace is sufficient for you." Know this about God—His words are genuine, which means His grace is enough for any sin and mistake, even the one you believe is beyond the reach of His mercy.

You will never fall so low that God's grace cannot reach you. Never. Let God's promise of His sufficient grace take root in your heart so you can walk in freedom and move forward with your life.

God says, My grace is sufficient for you.
Believe Him.
Walk in freedom today.

Remember there is grace for your mistakes and sins.

Write some things you need to let go of and pray about them.

Creative Writing

~ Just You and I ~

Rest Is a Must

And He said to them, "Come aside by yourselves to a deserted place and rest a while." For there were many coming and going, and they did not even have time to eat.

Mark 6:31

I used to believe that rest was unproductive. Then, I learned it was beneficial. You may have learned too that rest is good for the mind, body, and soul. You may now know that when you disconnect yourself from mental and physical activity and just allow yourself to be in a relaxed state, you are doing something important. You may now understand that rest gives your brain a break from its tedious, constant work and allows you the chance to gain clarity and regain mental and physical strength. Rest allows you to unwind and refresh.

Yet, for some of you, even knowing the benefits of rest doesn't erase your guilt from thinking of resting or actually resting. The idea of rest seems selfish. Getting you to believe that rest is unnecessary and selfish and that you should feel guilty for resting is a scheme of your enemy (Satan). If he convinces you that rest is idleness and selfish, then he has you on the right path toward burnout, emotional distress, unhappiness, resentment, and misery. He knows the benefits of rest, which is why he desires to persuade you that you are somehow not being a good steward of your time, or you are an ungodly wife or neglectful mother if you take time to rest.

The Creator of the Universe—God, rested. He did not have to because He is God. But He rested as an example to us that we must rest too. God worked for six days and took an entire day to rest. Jesus called the disciples and told them to rest a while. Rest is a gift Satan wants you to ignore. Instead of ignoring it, embrace it. Embrace it because you need it. You deserve it. You are entitled to it, and you are better when you rest.

Go to a place where you can rest a little while and enjoy needed time with yourself—*every day*—because rest is a must.

Remember to rest each day.

Identify three simple steps that you can take to ensure that you rest.

Creative Writing

~ Just You and I ~

Daniel Was Right

Because there is no other God who can deliver like this.
Daniel 3:29b

Years ago, a dear friend of mine spent the weekend at my home. Sunday arrived, and it was time to take her home. While alone in my car, waiting for my friend, I felt a strong urge from the Holy Spirit to pray, one I had never experienced before. Scared and confused, I asked, "what should I pray for?" I then heard the soft voice whisper, protection. So, I prayed for protection. The fear that something terrible would happen overwhelmed me, but we arrived safely at my friends' home. However, shortly after I departed her home, I had a severe accident.

My rate of speed around a narrow bend that I was unfamiliar with was too high, causing my car to spin and hit a concrete pole. When I regained consciousness, I realized that my car was facing the opposite direction to where I was headed. The weight of the car rested on my lower body. Tears began to pour down my face, and I screamed to God in physical and emotional agony and panic. I told God, "I don't want to die." Shortly after my desperate plea, a beautiful woman with brunette hair stopped to assist me. She tried to calm me as I hyperventilated — I thank God for her.

The seatbelt had slashed my chest, leaving a severe burn. My feet were trapped under the gas and brake pedals. Soon, the paramedics arrived, and I could see the worry on their faces. The team strategized the best method to remove me from my vehicle. Eventually, they used the "jaws of life" to rescue me. After several attempts, I was freed and then air-lifted to a local hospital with the worst assumed.

Following X-rays and other procedures, my diagnosis was only a broken ankle. Shock, awe, and gratitude flooded my soul. Hours earlier, I thought I was going to die, and then, I was on my way home. The police officer who came to the hospital said I was lucky I survived. He'd been called to that accident site many times with very few surviving. Daniel was right. *There is no other God who can deliver as the Father!*

Remember a time when God rescued you.

Tell someone about a time God rescued you.

Creative Writing

- Just You and I -

Pray Them Home

Pray without ceasing.

1 Thessalonians 5:17

A minister spoke at my late cousin Richard's funeral to a crowd of primarily youth. We gathered to celebrate the life of a young man who passed at the tender age of nineteen. The minister's sermonette highlighted that Richard set his heart right with the Lord before he died.

As we all have, Richard wandered from the commands of God. However, in time, he found that God, and not things of the world, could satisfy him. God, knowing all things, fought for Richard's heart and won before it was too late. Through his struggles, Richard's family never stopped praying for him. They prayed fervently that he would rededicate his life to the Lord. His family demonstrated unconditional love and support towards him.

Mothers, *never* stop praying for your children. Lift them in prayer to God who answers prayers. Whether in your closet, at your workplace, or on your knees, pray without ceasing. Bring their names to the Lord even when your hearts are tired and worn. Even when it seems in vain, still pray. Keep on praying that God will transform their hearts. He remembers and loves your children, so do your part as mothers and pray them home.

This devotion is dedicated to the Dunn family. Thank you for allowing me to share Richard's story.

Remember that God has not forgotten your child.

Pray for your own or someone else's child daily.

Creative Writing

- Just You and I -

Trust God to Direct You

Trust in the Lord with all your heart, and lean not on your own understanding; in all your ways acknowledge Him, and He shall direct your paths.

Proverbs 3:5–6

We have all been there— "This new supervisor will be less demanding;" "This move will make things better;" "This church will have fewer problems." Oh, yes! Time and time again, we have found ourselves in the valley of decision because we're desperate to move. In our desperation, we make sudden decisions, believing that life will be better, yet things don't turn out the way that we hoped or imagined.

Sometimes our situations are distressing, and we want to move forward. Aspiring to make changes to create a better life for ourselves is commendable. We are destined to achieve goals in life—ones that will create enjoyment, prosperity, and more. We are meant to achieve success and inner peace.

God values your happiness and inner peace. He wishes more than anyone for you to be content, whole, and successful. Your aspirations mean much to Him. What He wants is for you to trust Him to direct your paths. He asks that you put your confidence in Him, believing that He will never lead you astray.

Talk with God about all you hope to do. Share with Him your desire for change. He will show you what to do, always. Lean on His wisdom and not on your own understanding and until whatever change, blessing, or opportunities you may be seeking occur, blossom where you are. Make the most of it. See what God is doing because rest assured, He is doing something.

You haven't moved yet for a reason, so open your heart to see what God is doing. God will move you from where you are when the time is right. Trust in Him, and He will guide you on your path.

Remember to place your life in God's hands.

Write down areas of your life where you need God to guide you and pray about them.

Creative Writing

~ Just You and I ~

But God

"And lo, I am with you always, even to the end of the age."
Matthew 28:20b

One doctor said that I would not live to see my thirteenth birthday,
But God favored me.

People mocked and bullied me,
But God saw beauty and potential in me.

When life at times seemed unbearable,
God kept me.

When God instructed me to do something and I disobeyed,
He showed me grace.

When I sinned and felt too ashamed to pray,
God showed me love.

I have doubted God many times, yet He remained faithful to me.
For that, I am grateful.

When I hid my praise and worship to God because I feared what others would think, God continued to love me.

Through my mistakes, the heartbreaks, the trials, the lessons, the obstacles, and the accomplishments, God has always been with me and for me. God favors you, and God loves you. He sees beauty and potential in you. And lo, God is with you always, even to the end of the age.

Remember Matthew 28:20.

Write a prayer of thanksgiving to God.

Creative Writing

~ Just You and I ~

Creation at Its Best

Then God saw everything that He had made,
and indeed it was very good.

Genesis 1:31a

In six days, God created the heavens and the earth. He made all that was required to meet our needs and for us to enjoy: the splendor and brilliance of the sun, the beauty, and magnificence of the moon and stars; the tasteful herbs and tall, beautiful trees, exceptional creatures of a different kind—all were created by God, and indeed, He declared that everything was good.

The earth is still good. The fruits of His labor are still evident. Earth still has many beauties and splendors that have yet to be seen. Take pleasure in God's creation. See, taste, hear, touch, and smell what is around you. The beautiful mountains and oceans, the exquisite fruits, the birds that chirp, and the bright sunshine and breathtaking sunsets are all present. God made the earth for you. Enjoy it.

When was the last time you went for a nature hike, swam in the lake, or watched the sun set or rise? Money should not be a factor in you experiencing the goodness of the earth. Your Father made it for you to take pleasure in. Seize your chances to explore His earthly creation while remembering that, of everything God made, you are His most beautiful and valued creation. God declares you good. So, take pleasure in knowing that you are the epitome of creation at its best.

Remember that you are God's most beautiful and valued creation.

Choose one thing you can do to enjoy God's creation.

Creative Writing

~ Just You and I ~

Seek and Encourage

Then Jonathan, Saul's son, arose and went to David in the woods and strengthened his hand in God.

1 Samuel 23:16

Our youth are struggling. Like adults, they smile and pretend that they are doing fine and that life is good, when truly their hearts are hurting and they are struggling to cope with the various stressors and stages of life. Silently and sometimes audibly, they cry out for attention, empathy, and help, without a meaningful response.

We remember our youthful days, though there are some experiences we would like to forget. We understand what it means to be curious about our purpose and question our worth and maybe even God. We remember our first love and our first heartbreak, and our struggle to find our place in this world. And we have overcome, or perhaps we're still overcoming.

Our youth needs to know that they can overcome their challenges, and that we can help them overcome. We can share our stories, listen without judgement and to understand, be a godly example, and encourage and support them. Some of us are afraid to share our stories because we believe that they can't handle it, or that our stories will negatively influence them. But the truth is that our stories may inspire a new path, help save them from a poor decision, or help them heal. Our stories could help save their lives.

Jonathan did two meaningful things. He sought David, and he encouraged him. He did not accidentally or randomly encounter David. Encountering David was his purpose. Make encouraging our youth not your obligation but your purpose and mission. Just as David was encouraged by Jonathan, you will also make a difference. Do not underestimate the power of your encouraging words, kind deeds, time, resources, and efforts. Seek and encourage our youth. Accept them, encourage them, nurture them, and continuously pray that God will help them become happy, healthy, purpose-driven, successful, and godly men and women.

Remember to seek and encourage our youth.

Ask God to use you in a youth's life.

Creative Writing

~ Just You and I ~

Follow His Example

Walk as children of light.

Ephesians 5:8b

A childhood friend of mine had hopes of starting a new chapter in her life. From what I remembered, she was excited. I received a call one day that she died. The news was hard to believe. In an instant, my friend was gone. Had she known that day would be her last day on earth, perhaps there were changes that she would have made, people whom she would have forgiven, and dreams that she would have followed.

A tragedy such as this sometimes inspires reflection. We reflect on our mistakes, hopes, plans, and how we have lived our lives. My mind wandered about my friend's relationship with Jesus. She had a difficult childhood and as a young adult, the world's temptations attracted her.

Now is what we have. The occurrences of yesterday cannot change, and the next moments are uncertain. That leaves us with right now. With every moment we have, Jesus calls us to follow His example. He calls us to live holy. We never know the moment of our final breath. Let us live holy for Christ moment by moment, day by day. Let us walk as children of light.

Remember to live each day for the Lord.

Pray for someone who has not yet decided to give his or her life to the Lord.

Creative Writing

God Will Cover You

Also for Adam and his wife the L*ORD* *God made tunics of skin, and clothed them.*

Genesis 3:21

The story of Adam and Eve's fall lets us know two things: we cannot hide from God, and there is no need to. After Adam and Eve sinned, they realized their nakedness, so they hid from God and made coverings for themselves. The fig leaves made by Adam and Eve were not sufficient, so God clothed them with tunics, made with a thicker, stronger material that would be enough to cover them. God's covering was enough.

When we sin, we feel ashamed and vulnerable before God, and we believe, like Adam and Eve, that we can hide from God. So, we hide. We don't physically run and hide behind a tree or move to another city, state, or country. Instead, we stop praying. We stop going to church. Our morning and afternoon devotions lessen. We no longer join prayer lines, small groups, or Bible Study.

We become disconnected, discouraged, and stagnant. Satan has us right where he wants us like he had Eve where he wanted her. But then, God searched for her and covered her. Similarly, God searches for you and wants to cover you when you sin or make a mistake. The word cover means to protect, conceal, and provide shelter. God does all three.

He still looks after us. Sometimes He covers our mistakes. He also provides emotional safety and inner peace for us—that's shelter. God's mission when you fall is not to search for you to punish or condemn you. God's purpose is to redeem you and make you whole so that you don't remain in the condition your fall placed you in. God wants to cover you. God will cover you.

Remember, God will cover you.

Seek God's covering when you fall.

Creative Writing

~ Just You and I ~

God's Unexpected Ways

Be anxious for nothing, but in everything by prayer and supplication, with thanksgiving, let your requests be made known to God.

Philippians 4:6

Israel once experienced a severe drought causing not even dew to form on the grass. Food was scarce. Yet, God's servant Elijah was fed and hydrated. God commanded ravens to bring him bread and meat, and he drank from a brook. God came through in an unexpected way.

I believe that sometimes we forfeit encouragement, opportunities, and God's provision because we unintentionally and intentionally reject who and what He sends to us. We may reject the homeless man or woman, the overlooked speaker, or a child who God intends and wants to use to bless us. Sometimes, our pride gets the best of us. Sometimes, our ignorance gets the best of us. Sometimes, our doubt gets the best of us.

God is calling you and I to stay open. We must stay open to the paths that He chooses, the people whom He uses, and the different ways that He provides. After all, He is God. No person, creature, or thing is off-limits for Him.

Be anxious for nothing. God has got you covered, yet it is up to you to trust that and embrace that He can make a way out of no way.

If God used a raven to feed Elijah, be confident that He will take care of you, always. He loves you. Just stay open.

Remember, God provides different ways through different people.

Stay open to how God chooses to provide for you.

Creative Writing

~ Just You and I ~

God's Perfect Blueprint

For I know the thoughts that I think toward you, thoughts of peace and not of evil, to give you a future and a hope.

Jeremiah 29:11

Architects—even the most talented ones can and do make mistakes. God never makes a mistake, especially when it comes to the details and purpose of your life. God has designed the perfect blueprint for you of people to meet, places to visit, relationships to build, steps to take, purposes to fulfill, and dreams to bring to reality.

What I believe happens often is that God's blueprint doesn't resemble the one we've designed for ourselves. We envision being married by thirty and having a family by thirty-three, but we find ourselves at forty without a husband or children. So, we believe there is an error in God's blueprint. Somehow, God made a mistake.

There is no mistake in God's blueprint and your decisions don't alter it. Follow God's perfect blueprint for your life. But, to follow it, you must know what it is. How do you know what God's perfect blueprint for your life is? Just ask Him. Asking Him is the easy part. The true challenges are following the blueprint when it doesn't make sense or takes you out of your comfort zone. And the voices of others and our inner critic can be so loud, powerful, and distracting that it is hard to hear the voice of God and understand what He wants you to do.

Sometimes you believe that you know what God wants you to do, but you become discouraged and question your calling, dreams, and life because of the struggles that you endure. Cultivate a relationship with God, and you will know His blueprint for your life. You will become so attuned with His voice and character and desires for your life that you can discern decisions, opportunities, connections, and relationships that are out of alignment with His divine purpose and hope for you. When you have cultivated that relationship, your trust in God and yourself will grow so deeply that you can navigate and overcome doubt, discouragement, worry, and anything else that may come up as you live out God's perfect blueprint for your life.

Remember that God has the perfect plan for your life.

Pray that you will follow God's blueprint.

Creative Writing

~ Just You and I ~

What Does Your Heart Say?

"But lay up for yourselves treasures in heaven, where neither moth nor rust destroys and where thieves do not break in and steal."

Matthew 6:20

Jeremiah wrote, our hearts are deceitful and desperately wicked (Jeremiah 17:9). God is saying that our hearts are imperfect. They are sometimes driven by anger, pain, and resentment, which leads to trouble. Still, our hearts give us direction, elicit hope and empathy, and allow us to develop meaningful relationships, including with God.

The heart reveals our motives and where our passions lie. Sometimes our passion is inheriting wealth or fame. Sometimes our passion is gaining power. Sometimes our passion is buying properties, apparel, or accessories that money can afford, whether we can truly afford it. There is absolutely nothing wrong with wealth or accumulating properties and exquisite things. God does not discourage wealth. In fact, the Bible tells us that God blessed His children with wealth, properties, and other possessions.

What displeases God is when our hearts are so focused on things with temporary value that things of eternal value can't seem to find room within them. In other words, heaven and eternal life seem forgotten or distant to us. So, my question to you is this, if

God performed a heart check on you today, would He find earthly, temporary things as the focus of your heart and efforts or would He see that your heart is centered on heaven and eternity?

Let me encourage you. There is room for it all, but some things must take priority. What is your heart's priority? Matthew 6:21 says "*for where your treasure is, there your heart will be also.*" I hope your heart says that you treasure heaven and spending eternity with God more than you treasure earthly things.

Remember to focus your heart on heaven and eternity.

Reflect on your heart's priorities and if your priorities aren't in alignment with God's, today is a good day to reprioritize.

Creative Writing

~ Just You and I ~

Hold On

Weeping may endure for a night, but joy comes in the morning.
Psalm 30:5b

Joy is not always the result of a struggle ending. Sometimes, joy comes from looking at or perhaps even digging for blessings or things that we can be grateful for during adversity. I use the term digging because sometimes it seems that we must search hard to find something good amidst our exhaustion, depression, pending divorce, financial struggles, or other storms or challenges that are causing havoc in our lives.

Turn your attention to the havoc that Jesus' disciples faced. During a storm, to their dismay, Jesus was sleeping—*unbothered.* His posture teaches us two lessons. Lesson one: when Jesus is present in our storms, we too can and should be unbothered. We should be unbothered because we can rest in His unmatched power. Lesson two: His love for us will never put or allow us in a situation from which He cannot rescue us.

So, yes, Jesus permits or causes storms in our lives, but never for His pleasure or our pain. The truth is, we don't like life's storms, and we don't have to, but when they are over, if we are honest with ourselves, often we can say that we learned, changed, and healed. We realize that we can pick up the pieces of our lives and move on, even after our worst storms.

Until your storm ends, seek joy—*contentment in all things.* Seek joy even if you must dig for it and then live it. I hope you see that the storm that had you worried, upset, sleep-deprived, anxious, and overwhelmed was never more powerful than God or you.

Remember that all storms do end.

Listen to the song "This Too Shall Pass" by Yolanda Adams.

Creative Writing

- Just You and I -

Make Prayer Your First Resort

'Call to Me, and I will answer you, and show you great and mighty things, which you do not know.'

Jeremiah 33:3

Praying people can attest to two powerful truths about prayer: *prayer changes situations and changes us.* Prayer reveals our wounds and areas that we need to grow in. Prayer heals. Prayer results in direction and deepens our intimacy with God. Yet, despite the power of prayer, its effect is diminished, and it is underutilized.

Prayer is sometimes our last resort instead of our first. And I can't help wondering what would happen for us, in us, and through us, if that changed? What if prayer was used for everyday decision making, such as what to wear or cook and how to respond to an argument? What if we paused in our spirit to call upon God at any moment to ask or tell God to lead us?

What difference would that make in our lives? What difference would we experience if we consulted God about the man that we are thinking of spending the rest of our earthly lives with and to father our children? What if we sought God's opinion on whether we should leave a job, accept a job, or relocate?

Perhaps this has also been your struggle, but in the past, I have had a hard time grasping the truth that God has time to answer me about what cantaloupe is the best one to buy or what to wear on a first date. I believed that God had other important things to do and take care of. He had dying children to heal, broken marriages to fix, nations to restore to Him, and lost souls to save. But then I learned that I am God's most important thing and everything that matters to me matters to God. And then I remembered, God is God. He is the God that David wrote about in Psalm 121, the God who never slumbers nor sleeps, not because He has too much happening at once, but simply because He never needs to.

Everything about you matters to God, and prayer is your weapon to access His desires, opinions, power, and direction for every aspect of your life. The power that prayer has is not reserved solely for breakthroughs or healing. Prayer is for everything that has to do with you. My encouragement to you is this: always pray in the spirit, even for things that seem mundane, and always make prayer your first resort. Then, experience the mind-blowing, radical, soothing, and sometimes subtle, power of prayer.

R*emember to pray about all things.*

L*isten to the song "On My Knees" (there are several versions).*

Creative Writing

~ Just You and I ~

Cast Your Burden on the Lord

Cast your burden on the Lord, and He shall sustain you;
He shall never permit the righteous to be moved.
Psalm 55:22

One day, you may feel fatigued by an issue. Another day, you may have made a financial investment that you realized was a mistake. Your son may unexpectedly announce that he is no longer attending church. Your husband of twenty-five years may walk through your bedroom door and issue you divorce papers. The job you have sacrificed for may fire you.

What I love about Psalm 55 verse 22 is that it does not stipulate what burdens we can bring to the Lord. David, the Psalmist, encourages you to give any and everything to Jesus that burdens you. The word cast means to direct or place. In essence, Jesus is telling you to direct your burdens to Him, to put them into His hands.

I have experienced situations that rocked my world and made me want to disappear. For a while, I did not give those situations to Jesus. I tried to fix them on my own until I decided to embrace what Jesus meant when He said that His yoke is easy, and His burden is light. I now choose to bring my burdens to Jesus. Some, we will carry together. Others, He will carry by Himself. But, no matter what, I never have to bear my burdens alone, and neither do you.

Giving Jesus your burdens does not mean that they will be removed. The source of your burden may remain, but you will no longer feel burdened. Instead, you will feel free, have peace, and be empowered with strength and solutions to handle what you endure. Jesus invites you to bring your burdens to Him because only He can bring you relief, rest, comfort, and healing. As tempting as it may be, resist your desire or custom to bear your burdens alone. Instead, cast your burdens unto the Lord.

Remember to give your burdens to the Lord.

Give your burdens to the Lord.

Creative Writing

- Just You and I -

The Man He Can Become

But He knows the way that I take; When He has tested me, I shall come forth as gold.

Job 23:10

The Bible reveals that Jacob lived up to the meaning of his first name—trickster and deceiver. He deceived his family and took advantage of them to gain what his heart desired. Jacob sinned.

But Jacob came face-to-face with God one night, and with every fiber in his being, he wrestled with God. Jacob held on to God so tightly and did not let go until God blessed him. There is no doubt that he was tired and worn from fighting because of whom he was fighting, but something caused him to not let go.

One encounter with God changed Jacob. Then, God changed his name to Israel for *he struggled with God and with men, and prevailed* (Genesis 32:28). Jacob's name changed, and his character changed. No longer was he a trickster. No longer was he a deceiver, and God made a great nation out of him. With a repentant spirit, Jacob confessed to God that he was unworthy of all the mercies that God had shown him (Genesis 32:10a).

We cannot always foresee who others can become because of their mistakes. But regardless of how low a man you love or value falls, God knows who he can become. Israel's beginning was imperfect, but his end was good. If you doubt the power of your prayers or feel hopeless because of the path a man you care for is on, trust God and let Israel's transformation encourage you. *Pray for the man in your life because you never know who he can become with God!*

Remember the power of God.

Pray that your man's steps are ordered by God.

Creative Writing

- Just You and I -

The Whole Armor

Put on the whole armor of God, that you may be able to stand against the wiles of the devil.

Ephesians 6:11

Not a moment goes by without Satan trying to steal, kill, or destroy you. He has schemes that are unique to you to cause you to stray away from God, your calling, and your identity. He is intentional with his schemes. So, be purposeful in conquering them.

God knew Satan's agenda. Therefore, He wanted to ensure that you had the right spiritual weapons. First, God wants you to understand that you *wrestle against principalities, against powers, against the rulers of the darkness of this age, against spiritual hosts of wickedness in the heavenly places* (Ephesians 6:12). You do not wrestle against your husband or child, the disgruntled and mischievous colleague or neighbor, or the person seeking to enter your marriage. You are wrestling against your enemy, Satan. Knowing your enemy helps you to defeat your enemy.

Paul says specifically to put on the whole armor of God. This suggests that putting on the entire armor is the surest way to defeat Satan. If we wear only part of the armor of God, we leave ourselves vulnerable to the consequences of Satan's schemes. Partially wearing the armor isn't enough. So, put on the whole armor of God.

So, what's this armor that you must wear to have victory over Satan? Paul says:

Know the truths of God for yourself so that you may not be deceived
Stand firm on God's word
Present yourself morally correct
Read the words of God which give you peace
Take the words of God with you wherever you go
Have faith
Accept Jesus' gift of salvation
Protect your mind
Guard the avenues of your soul
And pray fervently.

Remember to wear the whole armor of God.

Read Ephesians 6:10–20.

Creative Writing

~ Just You and I ~

The Other Potter

Therefore, if anyone is in Christ, he is a new creation; old things have passed away; behold, all things have become new.

2 Corinthians 5:17

A human potter refines pieces, turning them into masterpieces. Jesus unravels and unveils existing masterpieces. One potter believes in an object's ability to become a masterpiece. The other Potter already sees His daughters as masterpieces. However, to unveil us, Jesus usually has the task of bringing down the walls that we have built from our traumas and pain. If we let Him, He will peel back our layers and show the world what He already knows and believes about us.

You are God's masterpiece. But, to bring you to life, He needs your permission. He must have your willingness to mold you—to bring to light some things that you have been hiding from and reveal beliefs and behaviors that do not align with the woman that He knows you are. There may be some tough lessons, tears, and resistance towards the unfamiliar, challenging, and uncomfortable molding process, but it is worth it.

The refining process makes you better. You don't have to love it, but I encourage you to not resist it. Jesus wants to finish the work of molding you that He started. You don't have to be afraid of what is to come and you do not have to fret about where you are because it is not too late for Jesus to mold you. Embrace where and who you are now, while being hopeful and excited about where you will be and your unveiling.

"Being confident of this very thing, that He who has begun a good work in you will complete it until the day of Jesus Christ" (Philippians 1:6)! If you have any reservations about what Jesus can do with you, put them aside. Give Him the chance to shape you. Let Him unveil you, His daughter, His masterpiece.

Remember that Jesus wants to and will finish the work that He started in you.

Let Jesus refine you.

Creative Writing

Crying Is Good

"Beloved, I pray that you may prosper in all things and be in health, just as your soul prospers."

3 John:2

Crying is a language. It communicates our frustration, anger, disappointment, our pain, and moments of joy. Sometimes, we cry, knowing the reason, yet we are sometimes swift to wipe our tears so no one will hear or see us.

When was the last time you hid or wiped your tears, maybe out of fear, shame, guilt, or regret? When was the last time you rushed to wipe your tears so no one would ask, "what's wrong" or "why are you crying?" You don't want to burden your loved ones with the burden that's burdening you. Instead of release, relief, and clarity, your heart is full of tension and anguish.

Crying is good for your soul. Crying expresses what words sometimes cannot. Crying liberates the soul and, sometimes, alerts you or someone else that everything is not as okay as you would like it to be or pretend it is. You have no reason to be ashamed of crying or the reason that made you cry. Even Jesus wept.

He was troubled and groaned in His spirit. Weeping expressed the agony that He was experiencing (John 11: 33 & 35). For some, crying is a weakness. For others, crying, like laughter, is medicine for the soul. How do you see crying? Do you view it as a sign of weakness? Do you view it as a source of release and relief? Do you see it as an opportunity to welcome someone into your heart's pain or struggles?

I understand that not crying in front of your child may feel like the best thing to do because you want to ease their pain. I know that sometimes you may have to dry your tears before you head into a boardroom to deliver a stellar presentation. And I understand that there are times when you may want to hide your tears to avoid worrying those you love.

I understand. Just remember this, crying is healing for your soul. If there are times when you feel that it may be best to wipe them, my encouragement is to carve some time to let them freely flow, even if it's just in the presence of God, because your tears are a language that God always welcomes and understands.

Remember: crying is good for your soul.

Cry as you need to.

Creative Writing

The Lesson from "Gossip Town"

"Finally, brethren, whatever things are true, whatever things are noble, whatever things are just, whatever things are pure, whatever things are lovely, whatever things are of good report, if there is any virtue and if there is anything praiseworthy—meditate on these things."
Philippians 4:8

The youth at my former church delivered a powerful portrayal of the skit *"Gossip Town."* By the title, you can guess the moral. While the lesson about gossip was powerful, the most salient message that I learned was about assumptions.

There is a famous cliché that addresses assumptions. Perhaps, what is worse than making a fool of ourselves is the pain, tension, and discord that we can cause when we assume. Assuming that our spouse or friend is ignoring us because of a slow response or that we are being gossiped about without credible proof comes with the risk of unnecessary hurt, anger, and turmoil within our relationships and souls. Assumptions disrupt our progress, productivity, and peace.

There is a difference between an assumption and instinct. I have learned to trust my instincts—internal cues that warn us when something is off. I believe that God speaks to us through instincts and we develop them, yet our instincts aren't perfect. We assume based on painful experiences, insecurities, and limiting beliefs. Betrayals from our pasts sometimes haunt us. When mistakes that we have made take root in our hearts, we can assume the worst about ourselves and our future.

Assuming can sabotage love, trust, and a strong bond. We should be careful about assumptions. The logical remedy is to seek facts, be present, and trust what we know. However, Paul offers a spiritual cure. Paul says to think of noble, just, and true things. Anything, he says, that is of merit and worthy of praise, think on these things. Paul knows assumptions begin with our thoughts. So instead of assuming, may we practice seeking the truth, being present, and trusting what we know, and above all, may we practice thinking about the things that are true, worthy, and good.

Remember Philippians 4:8.

Have you assumed something that you need to apologize for? If so, today is a good day to say I'm sorry.

Creative Writing

~ Just You and I ~

Don't Look Back

"But Lot's wife, from behind him, looked back, and she became a pillar of salt."

Genesis 19:26

Looking back isn't always accompanied by despair and anger. When we look at our pasts, sometimes, we gather strength from realizing that we overcame obstacles, made a significant change, or achieved a goal. Looking back at good memories can bring us joy. So, it is good to look back sometimes. The issue with Lot's wife is that she looked back after being told not to. There lies the danger. The danger is in doing what God commands us not to.

God instructed Lot and his family to leave their city and not look back. He tried to spare them from being destroyed. God planned to bring them to a better land. Yet, Lot's wife looked back and turned into a pillar of salt.

When God says to not look back, trust that He wants you to look ahead for a reason. Looking back can keep you stagnant, cause remorse, and evoke pain and doubt. Trust in what He has ahead even if you don't know what or who it is. If God always told us everything that He had in store for us, fear, doubt, and insecurities would possibly cripple us. The vision, spouse, or opportunity may scare us into inaction or reverting to the familiar because we feel unworthy of what God showed us.

Don't look back when God has told you to look forward. The past is familiar and sometimes tempting but what lies ahead of you is so much greater. Instead of focusing on the fear of the unknown or convincing yourself that you are unprepared or not enough, create a new narrative for yourself, one that says that you have everything it takes and you are enough, a narrative that is affirmed by your Father.

Remember to look and move ahead.

Read the story of Lot's wife in Genesis chapters 18–19.

Creative Writing

What's Your Foundation?

Unless the Lord builds the house, they labor in vain who build it.
Psalm 127:1a

Though physically occupied, there are homes that are spiritually empty because God is absent. However, He is not absent by choice. In a spiritually sound home, God is welcomed. Laughter, unity, and gratitude are present. Worship happens, and love and respect are in abundance. There is peace in the atmosphere.

Still, a spiritually sound home is not immune to problems. What is different is that the family members are more prepared to deal with issues because God is their foundation. The principles of God govern their hearts. What principles?

Be kind and affectionate to each other. Listen. Be slow to speak. Be slow to get angry. Forgive. Don't go to bed angry. Don't keep a record of wrongs. Do everything without grumbling or complaining. Pray without ceasing. Seek ye first the kingdom of God and His righteousness, and everything else will fall into place. Trust in the Lord with every fiber of your being and do not lean unto your own understanding. In everything you do, acknowledge Him and He will show you what path to take.

Examine your home today to determine if God is its foundation. If the results of your analysis indicate that changes are needed, be not ashamed or frightened. Instead, ask God to help your family to make the changes. And don't worry if any changes you hope to see don't happen as quickly as you'd like. Lasting change takes time.

God has a love for families like no other, and he wants your home and family to be spiritually fortified. He wants every home to reflect His character and experience His love and promises. God is the only One who can keep the spiritual foundation of your home strong. So, make God the center of your home.

Remember to make God the center of your home.

Pray that God will be the center of your home.

Creative Writing

Dear Daughter

The Lord has appeared of old to me, saying: 'Yes, I have loved you with an everlasting love.'

Jeremiah 31:3a

*ear Daughter,*

I am writing you this letter to tell you that I love you.

I adore you! I created you in My image and you are special to Me.

I sent My Son to die for you to save you from sin. That was the ultimate sacrifice, and it was worth it.

Life on earth is not always easy or fair but know that I am always with you. Through every trial and every heartache, I am there. I don't promise to remove every storm from your life, but I promise to carry you through every storm. You are my heartbeat. You bring me joy. There is nothing you can do that will make me love you any less—*nothing*.

I want the best for you in this life. Your happiness brings me joy. I have a purpose for you, and it is a good one. There is a home in heaven for you. There will be no more sickness, pain, sorrow, or tears. I am looking forward to the day when My Son brings you home! I look forward to you hearing, well done, my faithful daughter. There is a Book that writes of My unconditional love for you. Search and read it. It will broaden your understanding of how deeply I love you.

My daughter, *I love you with all My being. I hope that this letter gives you a glimpse of how much.*

With all My love,

Your Father

Remember, God loves you unconditionally.

Write a love letter to God.

Creative Writing

To Fear the Lord Is Wisdom

"The fear of the Lord is the beginning of wisdom, and the knowledge of the Holy One is understanding."

Proverbs 9:10

At one's first reading of the verse above, we may presume that the described fear is being afraid or frightened. However, the fear that the author talks about refers to reverence and admiration for God. When we revere God, we seek Him, and when we seek Him with all our hearts, we gain wisdom. We begin to discern why He does the things that He does.

We learn why we did not get the job that we prayed and worked hard for. We can accept why God allowed a man that we loved to walk away from us. We may realize that God allowed him to walk away because we would not have walked away on our own. Our perspective about life and death changes, and we see God in a different light, a better light. We figure out that every open door that seems good to walk through is not from God. We increase our discernment in relationships, business, work-life, and finances.

We usually don't value the opinions of those that we do not trust or honor. We do not usually make life-changing decisions based on advice from a person that we don't value or love. When you revere God for who He is, you trust Him as your source. He becomes your source of wisdom, peace, comfort, and change. The life-changing decisions that we face or even the smaller ones become easier to decide with wisdom from God, the creator, sustainer, and lover of our souls.

But wait, Proverbs says that there is more. We gain understanding when we know the Holy Spirit. The Holy Spirit, in the simplest yet most profound term, is amazing. He is a guide, advocate, comforter, and helper. When you know Him, things you were confused about will become clear, and you will understand not only God's will for your life but the seasons of your life and His will in seasons or situations. I now understand, through the Holy Spirit, that everything is not always what it seems at the first glance.

Remember, the fear of the Lord is the beginning of wisdom.

Seek God's wisdom.

Creative Writing

~ Just You and I ~

Let Love Be Your Motivation

And above all things have fervent love for one another, for "love will cover a multitude of sins."

1 Peter 4: 8

Sometimes, as women, we believe that we can save a wayward man. We may not say those words outrightly, but we show our belief by our actions. We may pressure him to come to church, chastise him with the word of God, or even silently pray that his heart is converted through a Saul-type experience. While God hears our pleas and sees our effort, He may not respond solely because some of our motives are not right. Our hearts are not in the right place.

Sometimes loneliness, our desire for marriage, and pride are the motivations for our prayers. We yearn to see a man saved because we desire him for ourselves more than we desire him walking in alignment with God's purpose and commands. A truth that may sting us and perhaps even stir our anger is the possibility that the man we are praying for may turn to God and walk away from us.

Sometimes, our motivation is love. Pray for the man in your life. Pray that he will be a man of integrity, wisdom, grace, and purpose and that he may walk closely with God for the rest of his days. Pray for him from a pure place. Show him the love of God. Live by example, and as the spirit leads, invite him to worship with you, pray with you, and study the Word of God with you. Whatever you do, let love be your motivation.

God knows the love you have for your love interest, partner, or husband. You have a common interest with God. Believe with your whole heart that God wants to save every man, regardless of how much he has strayed from Him or His word. Be the godly woman you are, letting love be your motivation.

Remember to let love be your motivation.

Let love be your motivation.

Creative Writing

Be Your Child's Example

Train up a child in the way he should go, and when he is old he will not depart from it.

Proverbs 22:6

Parents have the privilege and responsibility of raising, mentoring, and nurturing children, who can change the world. God's Word is paramount in helping raise children with integrity, compassion, and empathy. God's Word and continuous prayer are needed to help them cultivate and sustain healthy friendships and relationships and to achieve success and inner peace.

What is also crucial to your child becoming who God created them to be is you being their example. You are their first example of love, strength, integrity, and what healthy relationships look like. Don't take lightly the power that you have to shape your son's or daughter's identity, self-worth, and purpose.

Live out the Word of God in front of your child. Forgive when it is hard to forgive. Heal, although you have every right to be bitter or angry. Apologize when wrong. Show them the meaning of self-care, self-love, and healthy boundaries. As he or she grows older, especially in today's world, self-love and identity are important. Be kind to others and strive for peace with all men. Be honest and love others as Christ has loved you. Show grace to yourself, others, and your children when mistakes or sins happen. Be quick to listen, slow to speak, and slow to get angry, as James said.

In everything I wrote, notice I never mentioned perfection. Your child does not need or want a perfect mother. Your child needs and desires the best version of yourself, which sometimes requires healing, letting go of the past, grace, and self-forgiveness. Yet, understand that depending on what's happening in and around you, your best self will be different some days. Still, show up! Be your child's example.

Remember to be your child's example.

Ask God to show you ways to become more of the parent that you desire to be.

Creative Writing

~ Just You and I ~

The Power of Friends

...But there is a friend who sticks closer than a brother.

Proverbs 18:24b

Friends are God's blessings to us. He knew that we would need women and men in our corner to love us through our mistakes, cry and eat with us after our break-ups, speak life into us when we fall, and correct us with grace when we are wrong. Our friends are God's vessel when we feel unworthy of going to Him directly. Our friends are wise when we lack discernment about a relationship or opportunity. I thank God that He knew that we would need shoulders to lean on when life becomes too burdensome.

I have the best friends. You may believe the same because it's true. If so, give thanks to the friends that you have. Life gets busy. We have kids, get promoted, move 3,000 miles away, get divorced, or become empty nesters, yet we have friends who remain throughout the different seasons of our lives. Treasure your friends. Honor your friends. Pray for your friends. Genuine, trusting, faithful, and pure-hearted friends are gems.

However, some friendships end because of betrayal, jealousy, or someone evolving. Sometimes we pursue different lifestyles and paths, and friendships end. Still, knowing that we must, at times, let go of a friendship for the sake of our family, inner peace, growth, destiny, and walk with God doesn't necessarily ease the pain. If a friendship ends, rejoice over the good moments, laughs shared and lessons learned, and allow yourself time to heal and move on.

Still, treasure your friends and friendships that remain while being open to creating new friendships as the Spirit of God leads you to. And remember that your friends are sometimes confident and strong on the outside but may be falling apart on the inside because the weight of the world is sometimes hard to bear. Nurture your friendships with time, communication, and prayer. Be there for your friends as much as you can and love them with all your heart because friends are indeed a powerful blessing.

Would you pause for a few moments and pray for your friends?

Remember to treasure your friends and friendships.

Pray for your friends regularly.

Creative Writing

~ Just You and I ~

Comforter Is Who God Is

"I, even I, am He who comforts you."

Isaiah 51:12a

At times when hardships or struggles occur in our lives, reassurance is needed. Comfort is needed through an inspirational message, phone call, or embrace. Sometimes comfort comes from our physical needs being met.

Visualize a mother with a young child, displaced from their home and traveling alone through the wilderness without a designated place to go. That was Hagar's predicament. She wandered aimlessly and, eventually, her food and water ran out. In her distress, she lifted her voice to the Lord and wept. She needed to know that in her time of dire need she was not alone and God would help her.

God responded to Hagar's cry. He sent an angel who said to her, "Fear not, for God has heard the voice of the lad where he is" (Genesis 21:17b). The angel also said to her, "Arise, lift up the lad and hold him with your hand, for I will make him a great nation" (Genesis 21:18). Then God opened Hagar's eyes. She saw a well of water, from which she and her son drank until they were full.

In her time of distress, God met Hagar's need. She found the comfort she desired. God provides in a wilderness and comforts everyone regardless of what their needs are. He asserts, "I am He who comforts you!" Your situation may be far different from Hagar's. Even so, the same God who comforted her will comfort you.

Remember that God will comfort you.

Ask God to comfort you in your time of need.

Creative Writing

Love Your Enemies

"But I say to you, love your enemies, bless those who curse you,
do good to those who hate you, and pray for those
who spitefully use you and persecute you."

Matthew 5:44

Loving others despite any wrong they have done to us is what Jesus commands. If we only love those who love us, what reward will we have (Matthew 5:46a)? As Jesus loves us endlessly, we are to love others—including our enemies. He shows us how to love our enemies in 1 Corinthians 13.

Be kind to your enemies in words and deeds.
Be patient with your enemies.
Do not be envious of your enemies.
Do not boast in front of your enemies.
Do not be prideful to your enemies.
Do not dishonor your enemies.
Do not be selfish to your enemies.
Be slow to anger with your enemies.
Do not keep score of your enemy's wrongs.
Do not delight if evil happens to your enemies.

1 Corinthians 13 verse 7 says, "love protects, trusts, hopes, and perseveres." And I believe it means that if we see evil happening, even to an enemy, our nature should be to protect them as the Spirit leads. We should trust their actions but also God's power to change them. We should hope for the best for them. Love for your enemies should never cease regardless of what's been done to you because your love is not conditioned upon their treatment of you. You love your enemies because Jesus Christ has instructed you to. So, although easier said than done, whatever comes your way, love your enemies.

Remember to love your enemies as Christ loves you.

Be good to your enemies.

Creative Writing

~ Just You and I ~

To Love the Lord

"You shall love the Lord your God with all your heart, with all your soul, and with all your might."

Deuteronomy 6:5

Without understanding the context of Deuteronomy 6:5, one may view God as an authoritative Creator demanding or perhaps forcing His children to love Him with all their hearts, souls, and might. Yet, this is not the case. The verse stems from Israel's wavering in their obedience and love to God. Their obedience and love to God were inconsistent, and God was essentially saying, "if you are going to love me, love me completely, with all your hearts, souls, and might, not half-heartedly. Be all in or not at all."

God's call to be all in or not at all is also for you and I. God can handle our waywardness, imperfections, sins, and past, and He can choose to deal with our inconsistency. But, as in a relationship where inconsistency in love abounds, so does frustration, distrust, chaos, and unfulfillment. God does not need our love. He desires it and wants us to be all in with Him because that is how oneness is cultivated, trust grows, blessings unfold, and transformation happens.

Are you at a crossroads?
Do you find yourself loving God half-heartedly?

The beauty of God issuing such a call as in Deuteronomy 6:5 is understanding that He never calls us to failure. God knows that loving Him with all your heart, soul, and might requires you to let go of some perspectives, habits, and maybe even relationships, and it is a struggle. The good news is that God is equipped for your struggles, but it rests with you to decide if you are going to love Him with all your heart, all your soul, and all your might.

Remember that you can love the Lord, your God, with all your heart, soul, and might.

Write in the creative writing section any struggle in loving God completely and ways you can overcome.

Creative Writing

~ Just You and I ~

Will You Be One Woman's Key?

Sing to the Lord, all the earth; proclaim the good news of His salvation from day to day.

1 Chronicles 16:23

Jesus Christ met the needs of those around Him. He fed the hungry, visited and healed the sick, and talked with those who needed a friend. Jesus had a heart for ministry and shared hope. His kind and gentle spirit opened the hearts of many to receive His news about *salvation.*

How did you first hear that Jesus saves you from your sins? Where were you when you first heard this? How did you feel to know that salvation was available to you? What was your life like before you knew it existed?

There is a woman who does not know about the saving power of Jesus. There is a woman who does not believe that she is worthy of being saved. Somewhere, a woman thinks that her life now is as good as it gets. The truth is many women need to know about salvation, but the thought of talking to many women about it, even though it's good news, may seem overwhelming and frightening. Rest assured, I understand.

Will you be one woman's key and share the good news of salvation? You could tell her your story. Maybe she lives in your household or is within your inner circle. Perhaps, the woman is your colleague or goes to your church. She may be the woman who seems to have it all together.

Somewhere, a woman is silently, privately, or publicly seeking hope for her sins and struggles. And while you are not her hope, you are her key to knowing the Source of hope and salvation. So, be bold; be brave; and be one woman's key. You would change her world.

Remember to be one woman's key.

Share the good news of salvation with another woman this week.

Creative Writing

~ Just You and I ~

Two Becoming One

"And the two shall become one flesh'; so then they are no longer two, but one flesh. Therefore what God has joined together, let not man separate."

Mark 10: 8-9

"Do you take this woman to be your lawfully
wedded wife?"
"I do," says the anxious husband.
"Do you take this man to be your lawfully wedded husband?"
"I do," says the merry bride.

From the moment couples say *I do*, their lives as husband and wife begin. Essentially, their journey of becoming one begins. A positive transition is prayed for and desired, but as some of you can testify, the road to blending two hearts and two families is not always smooth.

Challenges from religious, cultural, socioeconomic, and personality differences emerge. Some challenges stem from unhealed childhood wounds, differences in strictness or boundaries, and unrealistic expectations, while others arise because of unforgiveness, pride, and lack of grace, compassion, and empathy.

Whatever challenge you face within your marriage, God has the solution. The solution may be therapy, vulnerability, or change within yourself, your spouse, or both of you. Seek God's direction. Trust that He will strengthen you, give you peace, and show you what steps to take as you handle any challenge. Pray for yourself daily. Pray for your husband, marriage, and family daily. May God's blessings be upon you and your family as you and your spouse become one.

Remember becoming one is a journey and God has the solutions.

Always pray for you, your husband, marriage, and family.

Creative Writing

~ Just You and I ~

Beauty in His Eyes

Do not let your adornment be merely outward—arranging the hair, wearing gold, or putting on fine apparel—rather let it be the hidden person of the heart, with the incorruptible beauty of a gentle and quiet spirit, which is very precious in the sight of God.

1 Peter 3:3–4

A woman of a gentle and quiet spirit is many things: courteous, calm, slow to anger, slow to speak, and quick to listen. She is humble. She is wise, compassionate, empathetic, and knows when to speak and when to remain silent. However, she must not be misunderstood or mistaken as passive or weak.

You may be privileged to know such a woman. You may consider yourself a woman of a gentle and quiet spirit, or perhaps you are striving to become that woman. Becoming that woman is not easy. We are imperfect and may still have some childishness within us. What's most important, though, is our desire and effort to grow into a woman of a gentle and quiet spirit.

Yes, outward adornment matters and feels good to our souls, so we should do our hair and wear our favorite polish. We should dress up and take ourselves on a date. What also feels good to our souls and matters most is when our character aligns with our outward beauty.

Strive to be a woman of a gentle and quiet spirit. When your outward beauty fades, your character remains. True beauty goes beyond how you look and reflects you. As we age, surgery, makeup, and accessories do not always conceal what we hope to hide, including an ungodly spirit.

There is beauty that lasts and is honored by God—the beauty of a gentle and quiet spirit. Take care of yourself physically, but also nurture your soul so you can experience and others can see what beauty is.

R*emember: a gentle and quiet spirit is precious to God.*

L*ook up the definitions of gentle and quiet.*

Creative Writing

The Lord Will Fight for You

"The Lord will fight for you, and you shall hold your peace."
Exodus 14:14

Holding our peace during a war on our character, relationships, business, or health is not our first instinct. Our nature is to fight. Yet, Exodus 14:14 tells us that we must hold our peace. What exactly does this mean? I understand it to mean "remain still and calm."

What an irony! Though ironic from a human perspective, from a spiritual standpoint, there should be joy, relief, and gratitude. Our stillness does not mean defeat and holding our peace reflects trust in God and patience.

It is hard to stand back and allow God to fight for us, not necessarily because we doubt His authority or love for us, but because His ways differ from ours, so does His timing. But, if we believe that He will fight for us, despite how our situation looks, we can be assured that God will fight for us. Be assured that God will fight for you, and if He desires your actions, He will let you know.

As tempting as it may be, resist the desire to fight your battles on your own. Resist the advice of others to take matters into your own hands or to get even. When we take situations into our own hands, things don't turn out well, and we often find ourselves overwhelmed, discouraged, and lost. Abandon your idea of victory and see victory from God's perspective. So, let God fight your battles for you in whatever way He chooses to fight them, and you—hold your peace.

Remember to let God fight all your battles for you.

Invite God into your battles.

Creative Writing

~ Just You and I ~

Favorites

~ Just You and I ~

Made in United States
Orlando, FL
16 May 2025

61314557R00100